PICASSO

I the King, *Yo el rey*

by Carmen T. Bernier-Grand   ◆   illustrated by David Diaz

Amazon Children's Publishing

ACKNOWLEDGMENTS

My thanks to Oregon Literary Arts for the fellowship that allowed me to research Picasso in Southern France and Spain; to my husband, Jeremy Grand, who drove me from Cadaqués to Côte d'Azur, from Côte d'Azur to Aix-en-Provence, from Aix-en-Provence to Gósol; to poet Carolyne Wright for letting me sit in her Whidbey Island MFA class; to Dianne and Alan Wade for the wonderful information they brought me from A Coruña; and to my French translator, Lisette Bernier-McGowan.

To my manita Lisette and my manito Segun
—C.T.B-G

For Toldie and Tater
—D.D.

The author gratefully acknowledges permission for the following paintings by Pablo Picasso reproduced in this book:
© 2011 Estate of Pablo Picasso / Artists Rights Society (ARS), New York

Picasso, Pablo (1881-1973) © ARS, NY. Portrait of the Painter Georges Braque, 1909-1910. Oil on canvas, 61 x 50 cm. Photo: Jens Ziehe. Nationalgalerie, Museum Berggruen, Staatliche Museen, Berlin, Germany. Photo Credit: bpk, Berlin / Nationalgalerie, Museum Berggruen, Staatliche Museen / Photo: Jens Ziehe / Art Resource, NY

Picasso, Pablo (1881-1973) © ARS, NY. Guernica. Paris, June 4, 1937. Oil on canvas, 349.3 x 776.6 cm. Museo Nacional Centro de Arte Reina Sofia, Madrid, Spain. Photo Credit: Erich Lessing / Art Resource, NY

Picasso, Pablo (1881-1973) © ARS, NY. Woman Ironing, 1901. Oil on canvas, mounted on cardboard. 19 ½ x 10 1/8 in. (49.5 x 25.7 cm). The Metropolitan Museum of Art, Alfred Stieglitz Collection, 1949 (49.70.2). The Metropolitan Museum of Art, New York, NY, U.S.A. Image copyright © The Metropolitan Museum of Art. Image source: Art Resource, NY

Picasso, Pablo (1881-1973) © ARS, NY. Gertrude Stein, 1906. Oil on canvas, H. 39-3/8, W. 32 in. (100 x 81.3 cm). Bequest of Gertrude Stein, 1946 (47.106). The Metropolitan Museum of Art, New York, NY, U.S.A. Image copyright © The Metropolitan Museum of Art. Image source: Art Resource, NY

Picasso, Pablo (1881-1973) © ARS, NY. Les Demoiselles d'Avignon. Paris, June-July 1907. Oil on canvas, 8' x 7' 8" (243.9 x 233.7 cm). Acquired through the Lillie P. Bliss Bequest. © Estate of Pablo Picasso / Artists Rights Society (ARS), New York. The Museum of Modern Art, New York, NY, U.S.A. Digital Image © The Museum of Modern Art/Licensed by SCALA/Art Resource, NY

Amazon Publishing

Attn: Amazon Children's Books

P.O. Box 400818

Las Vegas, NV 89149

www.amazon.com/amazonchildrenspublishing

Library of Congress Cataloging-in-Publication Data

Bernier-Grand, Carmen T.
  Pablo Picasso : yo el rey = I the king / by Carmen T. Bernier-Grand ; illustrated by
      David Diaz. — 1st ed.
      p. cm.
  In English.
  ISBN 978-0-7614-6177-7 (hardcover) —ISBN 978-0-7614-6179-1 (ebook) 1.
      Picasso, Pablo, 1881-1973—Biography—Juvenile literature. I. Diaz, David. II.
      Title.
  N6853.P5B48 2012
  709.2—dc23
  [B]
  2011032177

The illustrations are rendered in acrylic, charcoal, and varnish on masonite board.
Book design by Patrice Sheridan
Editor: Margery Cuyler

Printed in China (W)
First edition
1 3 5 6 4 2
Amazon Children's Publishing

CONTENTS

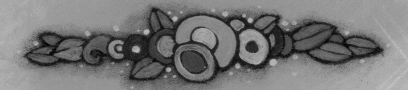

"My grandfather was a Sun King, a fixed point in the firmament, around whom women moved like planets in perpetual orbit, sometimes coming closer, other times drifting further away— assuming that he had not banished them to burn out at the far end of the universe."

—Oliver Widmaier Picasso

"Painting is poetry
and is always written in verse
with plastic rhymes,
never in prose."

—Pablo Picasso

A PRODIGY

When he was a child,
his mother told him:
"If you become a soldier,
you will be a general.
If you become a priest,
you will be the Pope."
Instead he became an artist,
an artist named Pablo Picasso.

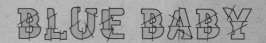

BLUE BABY

Málaga, Spain
Tuesday, October 25, 1881

11:15 P.M.
Pablo Picasso is born blue.
Fails to breathe. Fails to cry.
His *tío* blows cigar smoke into his nose.
Pablo makes a face and wails.

November 10, 1881
Parroquia de Santiago

He is christened
Pablo Diego José Francisco de Paula
Juan Nepomuceno María de los Remedios
Cipriano de la Santísima Trinidad
Ruiz y Picasso.

In front of the church,
his godfather tosses silver coins.
May the godson live the life of the rich.

SUN KING

"An angel and a devil in beauty,"
  Mama says.
"No one can cease looking at him!"
Mama, *Abuela*, and two *tías*
orbit around their Sun King.

"*Piz.*" *Lápiz.* Pencil.
Each time he draws a spiral,
the women give him a syrupy,
spiral-shaped *torrija.*
He fills entire pages with spirals,
fills his belly with *torrijas.*

MAMA:
DOÑA MARÍA PICASSO
Y LÓPEZ

Pablo inherits her looks.
A *malagueña*,
so small her feet do not touch
the ground when sitting.
Coal black hair,
a little mole over her upper lip.
Her dark eyes rarely blink,
polished black mirrors reflecting
Pablo.

PAPA:
DON JOSÉ RUIZ Y BLASCO

So tall his hand rests on top of wardrobes;
So blue his eyes, ivory skin; dark-blond beard.
People called him "The Englishman."

Papa takes Pablo to La Malagueta.
Slower than slowly, Pablo traces
the embroidered silver and gold
on torero Cara Ancha's *traje de luces*.

From then on,
Pablo paints *picadores* and *matadores*.

Papa paints dining room pictures
with pigeons and partridges,
hares and rabbits, fur and feathers,
fowl and flowers,
but mostly pigeons and lilies,
lilies and pigeons.

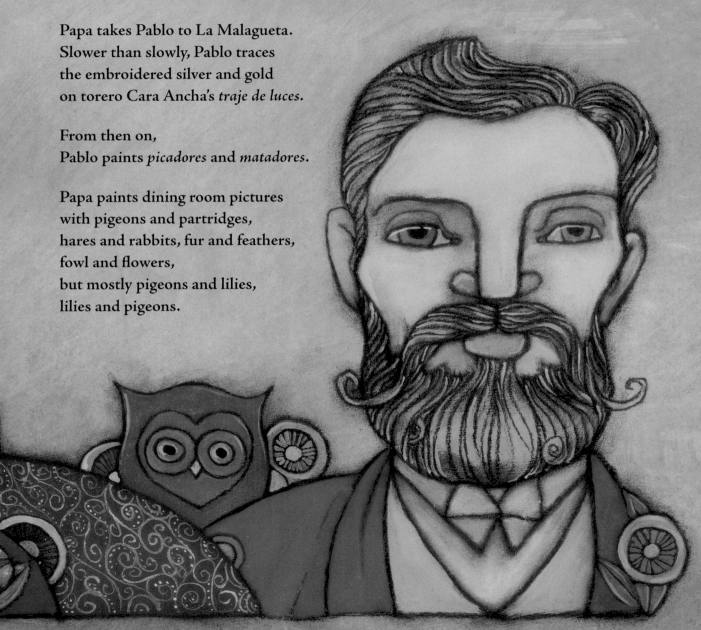

IN THE MIST OF AFTERSHOCKS

8:55 P.M., Christmas 1884

¡Triquitraque-triquitraque-triquitraque!
Mama's eyes open to perfect circles.
¡Tan! ¡Tan! ¡Tan! toll the church bells.
E-a-r-t-h-q-u-a-k-e!
Mama ties a scarf under her chin.
Papa flings his cape over his shoulders,
    bundles Pablo in its folds.
    Out! Out! Out!
People in the street screaming,
    streaming like a river running over its bank.
Houses crumble.
Papa hurries his family
    to an artist's stone house.

Three days later, in the midst of aftershocks,
    Lola is born.
Pablo clings to Papa.
    Pablo has been dethroned.

ARITHMETIC ART

Pay attention in school,
and Papa will let you paint a picture in oil.
¡Vale! Pablo sits as still
as a pigeon with clipped wings.

Arithmetic does not sink in.
On a sheet of paper,

0   is the eye of a pigeon
1   a person in the distance
2   a pigeon wing
3   butts or breasts
6   a wineskin
8   head on body
9   a flower

HIS AUDIENCE

October 30, 1887

Conchita is born.
Mother-of-pearl skin, like a *concha*.
Mediterranean blue eyes, like the sea.
She sits in Pablo's audience.
"What do you want me to cut out?"
    Sometimes a cock,
    Sometimes a neighbor,
    Sometimes a dog.
Pablo folds a sheet of paper fast several times,
cuts it out with *tía* Eloisa's embroidery scissors.
Each clip makes Conchita's eyes flicker.
Clip-clip-clip, a furry chin. *Clip-clip*, an eye.
Unfold the paper, please. A dog!
Pablo is a magician!

VOW TO GOD

Grapes turn to raisins under the sun.
Papa moves his family
from Málaga to A Coruña.
The rain turns their days into sorrow.
Conchita can't breathe.
Death oozes out of her eyes.
Diphtheria.
"God," Pablo prays,
"I vow never to paint or draw again,
as long as you let my beloved Conchita live."
The white linens stop rustling.
The first sounds of wailing are heard.
God has decided:
Conchita is dead.

SET HIM FREE

Papa moves his family to Barcelona,
teaches at La Llotja School of Fine Arts,
enrolls Pablo to win awards for pious paintings.
First Communion. Science and Charity.
Nuns commission copies of altarpieces by Murillo.
"The idea bores me, so I copy them up to a point,
then rearrange things according to my own ideas."
Papa and *tío* Salvador send Pablo to Madrid's
Real Academia de San Fernando.
Pablo wakes up at noon, walks to Retiro Park,
fills sketchbook after sketchbook—
bullfights, lovers in the park, street fights.
He strolls on torn streets seeking ladies of the night.
Papa writes, "You're taking the wrong road."
What a cold winter! Pablo falls ill.
Scarlet fever. Death prowling. Empty eyes.
On a straw mattress in his garret in calle Zurbano,
he draws…cup…hat…chamber pot…shoes…ant.
Empty pockets. Tío no longer sends money.
Pablo's Madrid freedom comes to an inglorious end.

GYPSY BOY

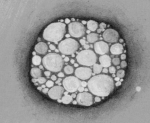

"Whatever I know I learned in Horta."
A gypsy boy teaches Pablo to chop firewood,
to sleep in a cave,

to take showers under a waterfall,
to understand bird songs.
"Whatever I know I learned in Horta."

Pablo spends eight months in Horta de Ebro,
black chalking and painting
and sleeping in a cave.

He learns to love
the miracle of dawn and goat herding.
"Whatever I know I learned in Horta."

Gypsy Boy vanishes into the night.
Never again will Pablo sleep in a cave.

I THE KING

Barcelona is dying with the century,
horrible, a black corsage.
In a large ledger turned sketchbook, Pablo writes,
"One portrait: 10 *pesetas*; three drawings: ten *pesetas*.
Received 0, 00 *pesetas*; struggle for 20 *pesetas*."
He burns his drawings to warm himself.

Parisian breezes blow from the north.
In Paris, Pablo can wear top hats,
red roses on his lapel.
Before his departure,
he paints his self-portrait, signs it "*Yo*."
He draws a couple on a sofa, signs it:
"*Yo el rey*." Underlines it. "*I the King*."

MELANCHOLIC BLUE

A candle in the neck of a bottle,
a handful of small brushes,
a pair of pliers
plucking lines from cardboard
(no money for canvas).
Pablo crowds rickety walls,
a family of pictures
in melancholic blue.

Woman Ironing (1901). The Metropolitan Museum of Art, New York, New York.

Three years later, Picasso painted a larger version of this exhausted woman bowing over the ironing board. That Blue Period painting from 1904 is at the Solomon R. Guggenheim Museum in New York, New York.

LA BELLE FERNANDE

Pablo moves to Bateau-Lavoir,
 a building shaped like the laundry boats on the Seine.

He sits in front of his apartment door.
His shiny chestnut eyes enchant
la belle model as she reads.
Mirada fuerte,
"You can have people with your eyes."
Mírame que ya miras
ya mírame que me miras

Black clouds break open.
Rush for shelter!
Pablo stretches his Siamese kitten
toward the perfumed arms of Fernande Olivier.
Inner fire. Magnetism.
She enters his studio.
She enters his life.
Rose colors enter his paintings.

GERTRUDE STEIN

A sale.

    Gertrude Stein—prose poet, art dealer, art collector, cubist of letters.

    She buys Pablo's painting, *The Little Girl with a Basket of Flowers.*

    "I am alone in understanding him," she says.

    "Perhaps because I am experiencing the same thing in literature."

Her portrait.

    "Nobody thinks it is a good likeness,

    but never mind, in the end,

    she is going to look just like that."

A change.

    "Little by little his drawing hardens.

    His colors become more vigorous.

    He is no longer a boy. He is a man."

Gertrude Stein (1906). The Metropolitan Museum of Art, New York, New York.

Gertrude Stein posed for this portrait eighty times. Before starting her face, Picasso told her that he didn't need her presence to finish the painting. Soon after, he went to Gosol, Spain, where artist Henri Matisse introduced him to African masks. When Picasso returned to Paris, he painted Stein's face to resemble a mask. She liked it.

LES DEMOISELLES D'AVIGNON

Picasso adorns brothel demoiselles only with skin.
Women dangerous as shards of broken glass;
African masked women
Intercessors
Against the unfamiliar
Against threatening spirits
To be feared
Fear of blinding syphilis
Fear of death

Les Demoiselles d'Avignon (1907).
Lillie P. Bliss Bequest @ Estate of Pablo Picasso.

This painting is considered the seed that sprouted into cubism.
But in 1907, critics thought the faces resembling African
masks were horrific and that Picasso was wasting his time and
creativity. Today *Les Demoiselles d'Avignon* is considered one
of Picasso's most famous paintings.

I PICASSO

"Every time I draw a man, involuntary I think of my father.
For me man is 'Don José' and that will be true all my life."
Don José. Not a man with a little boy anymore.
Now both are men, two different men.
Pablo has changed.
His signature has changed.
P. Ruiz
P. Ruiz Picasso
P.R. Picasso
R. Picasso
Picasso

Portrait of Painter Georges Braque,
(1909–1910). Nationalgalerie,
Museum Berggruen,
Staatliche Museen,
Berlin, Germany.

Picasso painted this cubist portrait
without a model, but he claimed
it was Braque who wore a
similar hat and smoked a pipe.
Braque denied it. In any case,
the eternal sadness of Picasso's
father can be seen in this face.

CUBISM WITH CUBES

Critics say,
"What a loss
for French art!"

But Picasso is not French.
Like Don Quixote,
he sees things.
They are not dreams.

Spanish villages are cubes.
His eyes catch pieces of summer on roofs.
He paints what he sees.

"I want an engineer to be able
to construct the objects
in my paintings."

Dripping with exhaustion, steaming with fatigue,
he destroys human beings, recreates them in cubes.
Neither past nor present helps.
He is alone with his terrifying struggle.

PIONEERS OF CUBISM

"Almost every evening,
either I go to George Braque's studio
or Braque comes to mine.
Each of us has to see
what the other has done during the day.
We criticize each other's work.
A canvas isn't finished
unless both of us feel it is."
Sometimes it is difficult for them
to distinguish one's work from the other's.
They support each other to the bitter end.

MADAME PICASSO

Picasso, an artist from Spain,
rises high, like the Seine!
He and Fernande move out of Bateau-Lavoir,
a furnace in summer,
an iceberg in winter where the hot tea freezes.
In their new home in Boulevard de Clichy,
Fernande calls herself Madame Picasso.
"Are you upset or sick?" she asks at his silence.
"I'm thinking about my work," he answers.
Give him quiet and a child to break the quiet.
They adopt thirteen-year-old Raymonde.
Picasso draws a human pyramid for Raymonde.
Picasso draws Frika and her puppies for Raymonde.
Picasso draws Raymonde.
Fernande returns Raymonde to the orphanage.
Never, ever will Fernande be Madame Picasso!
Soon their relationship ends.

CURSED

Picasso proposes to *Ma Jolie*—Eva Guel—
Fernande's best friend.
Eva accepts.
Fernande curses them.

Picasso continues to feel cursed.

Papa dies on May 3, 1913.
Picasso cuts up the newspaper
to make a portrait of Papa, his only master.
Picasso falls ill with dysentery.
Picasso's dog, Frika, dies.
Ma Jolie dies of breast cancer.
"I love you in every color," Picasso tells Gaby la Catalane,
his new lover.
JE T'AIME Gaby, he writes in six colors.
She refuses to marry him.
Picasso offers Irène Lagut a wedding trip to Rome.
This *novia* walks out on him.
What a curse!

GOLD CROWNS

As paint is to brush, women are to Picasso's art.
He follows ballerina Olga Khokhlova to Rome, Naples, and Barcelona.
The Ballet Russe performs Jean Cocteau's *Parade,*
with sets and costumes designed by Picasso.
Picasso paints:
    Olga wearing a mantilla over her saffron hair,
    Olga wearing a blue dress with a fur collar,
    Olga on a chaise lounge clutching a teddy bear.
A revolution in Russia, air raids in Paris,
food shortages, and blackouts:
World War I.

July 12, 1918

Olga and Picasso marry in Paris's Russian Orthodox Church,
wear gold crowns on their heads.
    A white-gloved chauffeur opens Picasso's car door.
    His trophy wife dresses in Chanel outfits.
    He wears suits designed by the best tailors,
    buys a Paris apartment and a Normandy château,
    replaces his bohemian friends with dukes and counts.
All he needs now is a scepter.

PAULO

At age forty, Picasso has a son!
Picasso paints
    Paulo riding a donkey,
    Paulo dressed as a harlequin,
    Paulo with a carved horse.
Son! Oh, my son!
Dame Olga busies herself with dukes, princesses, kings.

Paulo has a Russian nanny.
Paulo has a private tutor.
Paint will stain Paulo's double-breasted suits
if he visits his father's atelier.

Picasso slips a toy car into Paulo's hand.
Paulo rolls it around the bowl of soup.
Arms flailing,
Olga screams in some other language than human.

Picasso always keeps what belongs to him—
houses, apartments, ties, matchboxes, women.
He and Olga have much to take from each other.
He will keep Olga forever and ever. Amen.

TANGLE OF
AMOROUS LIAISON

Saturday, January 8, 1927

"Mademoiselle, you have an interesting face.
I would like to paint your portrait. I am Picasso.
I have a feeling that we will accomplish great things together."
Picasso? Who is Picasso?
He takes her to a bookstore, shows her a book about him,
walks her to a café for lunch, guides her to his studio.
Her face is a fruit bowl, her eyes peaches, her breasts green apples.
"Come back tomorrow." After that it's always tomorrow.
His sculptures undulate

    sinuous curves,

    serpentine arms,

    bionic movements.

Picasso wreaths Marie-Thérèse Walter
in tendrils of philodendron,
a plant of overwhelming vitality.

MAYA

September 5, 1935

Marie-Thérèse gives birth to a blue baby.
Picasso sprinkles water over her head,
whispers her baptism,
María de la Concepción,
after his dead sister Conchita.

Cieux! His baby girl springs to life!

    Picasso stays with his new family.
    He washes clothes. He cooks meals.
    He keeps a journal of drawings of his daughter.
    She calls herself Maya.
    Picasso paints:
    Maya wearing a red apron,
    Maya with her doll,
    Maya with a boat.
Maya is Picasso's work, but he cannot give her his name.
Olga will never divorce him.

MINOTAUR

Picasso,
a minotaur,
bull-man,
ravenous for orgies.
Maidens must sacrifice everything
to be immortal in his art,
and multiply his glory.

KNIFE GAME

Embroidered pink roses climb
the black gloves of Dora Maar.
A hand with fingernails polished in black grips a knife,
throws it, stabs the table between her outstretched fingers.
Closer.   Closer.
Faster. Faster. Faster.
Three gushes of blood.
Under her spell, Picasso writes:

Young beautiful carpenter
who nails down floorboards
with rose thorns
doesn't shed a tear
to see the wood bleed.

The Wicked One, she calls herself,
a surrealist photographer,
    a Scorpio like Picasso.

They both like danger and its rewards.

GUERNICA

April 26, 1937

Monday—market day
Guernica
Basque city
bombed.
Peasants shot from the air.
Children and women
horses, sheep, cattle
    slaughtered.
Terrible deaths.

Picasso paints:
eyes open in horror,
mouths shrieking,
a horse screaming,
a shocked bull.

Guernica (1937). Nacional Centro de Arte Reina Sofía, Madrid, Spain. Three thousand people died in the Nazi bombing of the Basque town of Guernica. More than a thousand were injured. The day after Picasso read about it, he began to make studies for the painting. Dora Maar photographed the process.

39

WEEPING WOMAN

Marie-Thérèse enters the atelier.
"What a surprise!" yelps Picasso.
Dora ignores Marie-Thérèse,
continues photographing the completion of *Guernica*.
May patience and silence
offer me their hands
May jealousy draw back its overbearing claws
"Well," Marie-Thérèse says, "things have changed here again.
I almost feel like a stranger."
"Come, come, my dear," Picasso says. "This is your home.
And everything is yours. *Guernica* is yours.
If you don't come to *Guernica*, *Guernica* will come to you!"
Dora wrings her hands, clenches her jaw. "Do you love me?"
"Dora Maar, you know that the only person
I love is Marie-Thérèse. That's all there is to it.
She is the one. We understand each other."
Marie-Thérèse pushes Dora out.
Marie-Thérèse's triumph means nothing.
Dora stops visiting. She waits for his calls.
Picasso often takes her to eat at Le Catalan.
The *ménage à trois* never ends.

WORLD WAR II

A sneering Gestapo raids Picasso's studio.
"Degenerate!" soldiers call him. "Communist!"
They kick his canvases.
Picasso gives the soldiers souvenir postcards of *Guernica*.
"Did you do that?" they ask, referring to the painting.
"No, you did," he answers, referring to the massacre.
"We'll be back," they say.
They don't return. It is not easy to arrest Picasso.

LA FEMME-FLEUR/
THE FLOWER WOMAN

Françoise Gilot.
What good fortune!
So young and a painter, too.
Her eyebrows like bird wings.
A new conquest, a new passion, a new style,
a new muse to Picasso's creative art.
He replaces features of his previous lover
with features of his current lover, until—
he asks Françoise to dress in mallow and green.
    Blue-stem body,
    Venus-blue flower face,
    verde-leaf hair.
"It's strange, isn't it? But it's absolutely you."

LOVE OATH

By a holy-water basin in a small church in Cannes,
Picasso tells Françoise,
"You're going to swear here that you'll love me forever."
"I can swear that anywhere," she answers,
"if I want to commit myself to that extent, but why here?"
"It's better done here than just anywhere."
She takes the oath.
He asks her to bear his child.

May 15, 1947

Claude is born.
Picasso paints:
    Claude taking his first steps,
    Claude sitting next to a chair where a dove landed.
Claude needs the sound of another child.

April 19, 1949

Paloma is born.
Picasso paints:
    Paloma and Claude playing,
    Paloma drawing with Françoise and Claude.

"I AM GOD"

"God is really another artist.
He invented the giraffe, the elephant, and the cat.
He has no style. He just keeps trying other things."
Picasso paints late into the night, an owl his only companion.

When Picasso has emptied himself of painting, he draws,
when he has emptied himself of drawing, he makes ceramics,
when he has emptied himself of ceramics, he makes prints,
when he has emptied himself of print making, he sculpts,
when he has emptied himself of sculpting, he illustrates,
when he has emptied himself of illustrating, he photographs,
when he has emptied himself of photographing, he writes poems,
when he has emptied himself of writing poems, Picasso paints.

An old wicker basket becomes the ribs of a goat.
A bicycle seat becomes a bull's head, the handlebars its horns.
Claude's toy cars become the head of *Baboon and Young*.
Picasso seldom titles his works.
Others do.
He has stopped signing his art.
What for? He knows who has done them.

"I am God…I am God…I am God."

ORBITING THE KING

Everything is his. He throws away nothing.
Everything must stay within his orbit—
his art, his cigarette boxes, his houses, his women.
Olga writes him daily letters
—long tirades in every direction—
horizontally, vertically, on margins,
in Spanish mixed with Russian and bad French.
Picasso gives her Château de Boisgeloup.
She moves from hotel to hotel,
stalking him like a specter along the shore.
Dora writes letters. "If you go on living as you do.
a terrible catastrophe will come down upon you."
He reads Marie-Thérèse's passionate letters to Françoise.
Their free love, the flight of a bird.
Marie-Thérèse's eyes, the Paris sky on a radiant day.
She is in his paintings, in his sculptures, in his engravings.
Françoise wants out!
"Why do you want to leave me?" he asks.
"No woman leaves a man like me!"
Françoise holds her children's hands and walks out the door.
They cross the bridge ahead of the wind.

BLANK CANVAS

February 11, 1955

Olga dies of cancer.
Picasso proposes to Marie-Thérèse.
She turns him down. "It's too late."
Françoise has married another artist.
Picasso's canvas is blank.

JACQUELINE ROQUE

"One can't leave that poor man alone
like that, at his age.
I must look after him,"
says Jacqueline Roque,
sales lady at Galerie Madoura,
twenty-seven-year-old sphinx.
She moves into Picasso's La Californie
with her six-year-old daughter Cathy.
Picasso paints:
    Jacqueline as a Turkish bride,
    Jacqueline dressed in candy-box paper,
    Jacqueline wearing a black scarf.
For the first time
Picasso does not mix in his canvases
the hair colors and the faces
of the different women in his life.

VILLA LA CALIFORNIE

In the summer, let the children just be children,
Claude, Cathy, and Paloma running to the clatter of palm fronds,
around the bronze she-goat and the man with sheep.
Let Paulo just be Paulo,
flying his Norton motorbike as if he wants to escape.
Let Maya just be Maya,
being her father's confidante, protecting the children from outsiders.
Let the family just be family,
Paulo, Maya, Paloma, Claude, Picasso attending *corridas* in Roman arenas,
children's hands on Picasso's head when the bull charges. *¡Olé!*
Let Picasso just be Picasso, blatting his bugle *ta-ta-ti ta-ta-ti, ti-ta-ta, ti-ta-ta,*
wearing an ancient African mask, humming zarzuelas when he forgets the lyrics.
In the summer,
let the salt of the blue-ink sea go into his nostrils and on his skin.
"This landscape belongs to me!"

BULLFIGHT

Picasso dips a slender brush in a dark solution of syrupy sugar.
Flick-flick. He paints left to right
the glistening mirror-smooth copper plate.
The Toréador song begins.
The matadores enter the bullring,
capes over their left arms,
chins raised, chests thrust out.
Few figures need more than one stroke.
The plate takes just a couple of minutes.
The bull's hooves churn the arena's sand.
A banderillero taunts the bull with his cape,
forces the bull to charge.
Go, bull, charge! *¡Anda, toro, faja! ¡Olé!*
The matador paces the bullring, daring the bull
to charge him.
The bull stands firm.
Next plate.
The bull swoops down on the matador.
The matador has made a mistake. "He made a mistake!"
With a rag of torn clothing, Picasso rubs out the matador.
Repaints him.
The matador has been flung skywards by the bull.

JACQUELINE'S SUN

March 2, 1961

Picasso orders his chauffeur
to stop in front of the town hall in Vallauris.
"I bet you can't guess what we're going to do here,"
he tells Jacqueline. "We're going to get married."
He is nearly eighty years old.
"I have less and less time," he says,
"and yet I have more and more to say.
What is important for me now is to be,
to leave the trace of my footsteps."
Jacqueline takes fierce pride
in her role as *Jacqueline de Vauvenargues*,
terrifying protector of her king.

Paulo comes to Château Vauvenargues
     to visit his father.
From behind the electric gate,
he hears Madame Picasso reply in the rain,
"The Sun doesn't want to be disturbed."

HOMMAGE À PICASSO

"Just what I needed, an homage show,"
Picasso complains.
"As if I ever accepted an homage in my life!"

"How was it?" Picasso asks photographer Roberto Otero
after the show opens.
"Tell me. Tell me everything."
"Absolutely hideous," Roberto jokes.
"Ah yes? I said it would be. You see, Jacqueline?
At last the truth is out about this whole Paris business.
I told you this would happen."
"There are a lot of paintings hung upside down," jokes Roberto.
"What a mess!" Picasso says, sitting in his throne-chair.
"I knew it would be like that."
Showing the catalogue of the exhibitions
held in Grand Palais and Petit Palais,
Otero tells him just *Guiterre* is hung upside down.
"To tell you the truth," Picasso says,
sipping "Queen of the Fields" herbal tea,
"even if they had turned half the paintings upside down,
what difference would it have made?
Basically, it is all the same, isn't it?"

BULL KILLS MATADOR

"I paint as others would write their autobiographies."
In a crowd of self-portraits,
Picasso pours out everything he feels,
his eyes expressing death, out-staring death.
Marie-Thérèse receives a letter.
His handwriting looks feeble. Is he well?
She calls him. He says he is really quite well.
He's lucid enough to work and shave.
He asks Jacqueline for paper and pencil.
Art is life. Boredom is death.
Bronchitis slides into his lungs, steals his air.
His days have messenger pigeon wings.
"Everything approaches on its own, including death."

April 8, 1973

The ninety-two-year-old matador confronts the bull.
The bull gores a deathblow to the matador's heart.
Pablo Picasso is flung skywards
from life into the immortality of kings.

PABLO PICASSO AND THE MISTRESS WHO NEVER LEFT HIM

"The painter Pablo Picasso died this morning in his house on the Côte d'Azur at the age of ninety-two. He is regarded as the artist who invented the twentieth-century art." On television, Maya's son, Olivier Widmaier Picasso, learned about his grandfather's death.

"He was born among the dead," says Widmaier Picasso, "and lived afraid of it when death prowled."

Pablo Ruiz Picasso was born a blue baby on October 25, 1881, in Málaga, Spain. His uncle blew cigar smoke on him and revived him. He lived ninety-two years, but he thought about death every day. "I think of it from morning till night—it is the mistress that never leaves you!"

When Pablo was ten, his father Don José lost his job as a curator of a small museum in Málaga and moved his family to A Coruña, where he got a job teaching at the School of Fine Arts. Soon afterwards his daughter Conchita fell ill with diphtheria. Pablo made a deal with God: he would stop painting if God would allow Conchita to live. Sadly, however, his sister didn't survive, and throughout his life, Pablo felt responsible for her death.

Don José moved the family again, this time to Barcelona, where he accepted a job teaching at La Llotja School of Fine Arts. He enrolled Pablo who won a gold medal for the painting *Science and Charity*. His uncle then paid for Pablo to study at the San Fernando Royal Academy of Fine Arts in Madrid.

Pablo hardly attended classes. Instead he roamed the streets, sketching and visiting the brothels until he fell ill and almost died of scarlet fever. To help him recover, his school friend, Manuel Pallares, took him to Horta de Ebro.

Pablo, once again in good health, returned to Barcelona and began to frequent *Els Quatre Gats* where he met Jaime Sabartés, later his secretary, and painter Carles Casagemas. Casagemas and Picasso moved back and forth between Barcelona and Paris. In Paris, art dealer Pedro Manach paid Pablo 150 francs a month for his paintings.

In 1901, Picasso sold fifteen paintings before the opening of an exhibition. But then Casagemas committed suicide, and that loss led Picasso to the work of his Blue Period. He painted poverty and loneliness in blue. Nobody wanted to buy these depressing paintings.

In October 1902, Picasso moved in with poet Max Jacob in Paris. Pablo could only draw because he had no money to buy canvases. After another trip to Barcelona in 1904, Picasso moved to Bateau-Lavoir in Paris, where he met model Fernande Olivier.

Picasso started to paint jugglers and acrobats in the Circus Medrano and Le Lapine Agile. He spent his evenings with poets Max Jacob, Guillaume Apollinaire, and André Salmon, and with painters Juan Gris and Marie Laurencin. They became known as *La Bande à Picasso*.

Thanks to Gertrude Stein and her brother Leo, who bought some of Pablo's paintings, and to Apollinaire, who insisted art agent Ambroise Vollard buy a few of Picasso's Rose Period paintings, Picasso finally began to work without financial worries.

But Picasso had no luck selling his early cubist painting, *Les Demoiselles d'Avignon*. Dealers, reviewers, and friends thought it was horrible, although today, it is considered among Picasso's most famous paintings.

Picasso wanted children, but Fernande became sterile after having an abortion. They decided to adopt thirteen-year-old Raymonde. But concerned that Picasso might have an affair with Raymonde, Fernande returned the girl to the orphanage. That prompted a brief separation between Picasso and Fernande.

Although Fernande had affairs with other men, Picasso's relationship with her didn't end until 1912, when she introduced him to her best friend, Eva Guel. He intended to marry Eva, but 1913 was a difficult year for him. On May 3, his father died. Then Picasso became ill with dysentery, and Eva was diagnosed with breast cancer. War was declared between France and Germany, and Apollinaire and Jacob enlisted. Picasso, a neutral Spaniard, stayed in Paris.

Picasso sat by Eva's hospital bed every day. But during that time, he also had an affair with Gaby Depeyre. After Eva died on December 14, 1915, Picasso proposed to Gaby who rejected him. Soon afterwards, Jean Cocteau asked Picasso to work in Rome on the sets for his ballet *Parade*. Picasso offered a Rome honeymoon trip to another paramour, Irène Lagut, but she also rejected him.

In Rome, Picasso met and proposed to ballerina Olga Khokhlova. They married on July 12, 1918. She traveled everywhere with her tutus and spoke at all times about ballet, but she never danced in public again. Their marriage ended Picasso's bohemian life for a while (she especially disliked Max Jacob) and almost ended his cubist art. Olga wanted him to paint neoclassical art because in Russia, it was what she had been taught.

On January 8, 1927, Picasso saw seventeen-year-old Marie-Thérèse Walter shopping on Galeries Lafayette. She didn't recognize Picasso for the famous man that he was, so he took her to a bookstore and showed her a book with his artwork.

In June 1930, Picasso bought Château Boisgeloup, near Gisors, north of Paris. There, he spent the week with Marie-Thérèse and the weekends with Olga and their son Paulo. Olga could see that Picasso's sculptures, paintings, and even his still lifes had become erotic. Even so, Olga felt young Marie-Thérèse didn't pose a threat to Olga's position as Madame Picasso.

On December 25, 1934, Marie-Thérèse told Picasso that she was pregnant. Under French law, a married man could not recognize his child if it were born to a woman other than his wife. On July 3, 1935, Picasso asked Olga for a divorce. She left their Paris home in rue La Boétie to live in a hotel, but she remained Madame Picasso until her death.

On September 5, 1935, Marie-Thérèse's daughter was born—a blue baby, like Picasso. Maya, as she called herself later when she couldn't say María, survived.

At the time that Maya was born, Picasso met surrealist poet and photographer Dora Maar, with whom Marie-Thérèse suspected he was having an affair. "I saw that Picasso was going out a bit. I understood why."

In April 1937, the Spanish Republican government requested Picasso to create a mural for the Spanish Exhibition Universelle in Paris. Following the Nazi air raid on April 26, Picasso painted *Guernica*, and Dora photographed his painting process.

On January 13, 1939, Picasso was wearing a red tie when he learned of his mother's death. Because he was superstitious, he never wore plain red again. General Francisco Franco's troops had entered Barcelona and Picasso had sworn he would never set foot in Spain as long as Franco's regime lasted, so he didn't attend his mother's funeral.

After the liberation of Paris on August 25, 1944, Picasso joined the Communist Party. As a member, he paid lip service but kept his distance, rarely attending meetings.

For weeks after the Liberation, Picasso was the "Man of the Hour." Many Americans went to visit him. From then on, it was hard for Picasso to live a private life.

That same year Dora underwent psychiatric treatment involving electroshock therapy. She never completely recovered. She turned into a religious fanatic and attempted to convert Picasso to her Christian beliefs.

For three years, Picasso tried to persuade artist Françoise Gilot to move in with him. Instead he moved in with her. Since his male pride didn't allow him to live in a house owned by a woman, he bought her house, La Galloise, near Vallauris.

Even though Picasso was a healthy man, he was a hypochondriac. He would tell Françoise, "My God if you only knew what sickness I have." But whenever Françoise got sick, he became as cruel to her as to his other women. When she was ready to go to the hospital to give birth to their daughter Paloma, he told her to call an ambulance because he needed the chauffeur. When she decided to leave him for good, he told her that nobody would marry her. He was wrong! She married the painter Luc Simon. Picasso also unsuccessfully sued her for writing a best-selling memoir, *Life with Picasso*. This rift distanced their children from him. Later he agreed that the book accurately portrayed their life together.

After Olga died in 1955, Picasso asked Marie-Thérèse to marry him. She declined. As he said, "The reward for love is friendship." They remained friends right up to his death.

Picasso knew a young woman, Jacqueline Roque, when Olga died, but it took him six years to propose to her. She agreed to marry him and took her role seriously as his guardian. She hardly ever let anybody come into the house, even his grandchildren.

On the morning of April 8, 1973, Pablo Picasso died.

"When I die," he said once, "it will be a shipwreck. When a large ship goes down many people in the vicinity are swept into the whirlpool."

The day after his burial on the grounds of Château Vanvenargues, his grandson Pablito swallowed a carton of bleach. He died three days later. On October 19, 1977, Marie-Thérèse hung herself from the ceiling in her garage. On the evening of October 15, 1986, Jacqueline shot herself in the temple with a revolver.

Pablo Picasso prophesized like a god. But he probably had no idea that Maya would become his art expert; Claude, his art's curator; his grandson Olivier, his biographer; his grandson Bernard, founder of his foundation and publisher; and Paloma, a jewelry designer. They proudly carry the Picasso name, and they hope that people will forgive Picasso's many faults and remember only *the* Picasso, the genius artist.

CHRONOLOGY

1881—On October 25, Pablo Ruiz Picasso is born in Málaga, Spain.

1884—His first sister, Dolores, known as Lola (1884-1958), is born.

1887—His second sister, María Concepción, known as Conchita (1887-1895), is born.

1891—Picasso's father moves the family to A Coruña, where he has been offered a job as a teacher.

1892—Picasso attends the School of Fine Arts in A Coruña and is taught by his father.

1895—On January 10, Conchita dies. Picasso's father moves the family to Barcelona. He teaches in La Llotja School of Fine Arts, where he enrolls Picasso.

1896—Picasso's *The First Communion* appears in an exhibition.

1897—Picasso's *Science and Charity* is awarded a gold medal in a competition in Málaga. His uncle sends Pablo to the San Fernando Royal Academy of Fine Arts in Madrid.

1898—Pablo spends several months in Horta de Ebro, sketching landscapes and regaining his health while recovering from scarlet fever.

1899—In Barcelona, Picasso frequents the café *Els Quatre Gats*, where he meets Carles Casagemas and Jaime Sabartés, later his secretary. Picasso makes his first sculpture, *Seated Woman*.

1900—At the beginning of October, Picasso and Casagemas move to Paris. Art dealer Pedro Mañach pays Picasso 150 francs a month for his paintings.

1901—Casagemas commits suicide in Paris. Picasso becomes co-editor of Madrid's magazine *Arte Joven*. In May he moves again to Paris. He sells 15 pictures before the opening of an exhibition at Ambroise Vollard's gallery. He signs his pictures "Picasso." This is the beginning of his Blue Period.

1902—Picasso lives in Paris with poet Max Jacob. Pablo has no money to buy canvases.

1904—Picasso moves to Bateau-Lavoir in Paris. He meets model Fernande Olivier.

1905—Picasso meets Guillaume Apollinaire, André Salmon, Juan Gris, Marie Laurencin, and Leo and Gertrude Stein. This is the beginning of his Rose Period.

1906—Picasso sells most of his "rose" pictures, enabling him to live without financial worries.

1907—Picasso finishes *Les Demoiselles d'Avignon*, his first cubist painting.

1908—Picasso and Fernande adopt 13-year-old Raymonde.

1909—Picasso and Fernande move to 11 Boulevard de Clichy, next door to Georges Braque. Picasso and Braque work closely together, developing the cubist style of art.

1911—Picasso begins his liaison with Eva Guel (Marcelle Humbert), "Ma Jolie."

1913—On May 3, Picasso's father dies. Picasso suffers from dysentery. Eva is diagnosed with breast cancer. War is declared between France and Germany. Pablo, a neutral Spaniard, stays in Paris.

1915—On December 14, Eva dies of breast cancer.

1917—Picasso goes to Rome to work on the sets for Jean Cocteau's ballet *Parade*. He meets Russian ballet dancer Olga Khokhlova.

1918—On July 12, Picasso marries Olga. They occupy two floors at 23, rue La Boétie.

1921—On February 4, Paul (Paulo), is born.

1924—Picasso paints Paulo as *Harlequin*. Picasso buys a car and hires a chauffeur.

1925—Picasso paints *The Dance*, reflecting the first signs of tension in his marriage.

1927—On January 8, Picasso meets seventeen-year-old Marie-Thérèse Walter.

1930—Picasso paints *Crucifixion*. In June, he buys Château Boisgeloup, near Gisors, north of Paris. In the fall, he installs Marie-Thérèse in a flat at 44, rue La Boétie, near his home and studio on 23, rue La Boétie.

1931—Picasso lives at the Château Boisgeloup with Marie-Thérèse.

1933—Picasso tries to prevent the publication of Fernande's book, *Picasso and his Friends.*

1934—On December 25, Marie-Thérèse tells Picasso she is pregnant. Under French law, if a child's father is married to a woman other than the child's mother, he can't recognize the child as his own.

1935—In May, Picasso begins writing surrealist poetry. On July 3, he asks Olga for a divorce so he can marry Marie-Thérèse. Olga denies him a divorce. Olga leaves 23, rue La Boétie and moves into Hôtel California. In the spring, Picasso meets Dora Maar in the café Les Deux-Magots in Paris. On September 5, Marie-Thérèse gives birth to Picasso's daughter Maya.

1936—Picasso works on his minotaur theme. On July 18, the Spanish Civil War begins. On September 19, the Spanish Republic names Picasso Honorary Director of the Prado. In Saint Tropez, Picasso meets Dora Maar again. Picasso gives Château Boisgeloup to Olga and moves with Marie-Thérèse and Maya to a house that art dealer Vollard has lent them.

1937—Picasso moves into a new studio at 7, rue des Grands-Augustins in Paris. Following a German air raid on April 26, Picasso paints *Guernica.*

1939—On January 13, Picasso's mother dies in Barcelona. On January 26, Barcelona falls to pro-Franco troops. On September 2, Picasso takes Dora Maar to Royan, France. The next day, war is declared in Europe. Marie-Thérèse and Maya join Dora Maar and Picasso.

1940—German troops occupy Royan and Paris. Picasso returns to Paris.

1941—Marie-Thérèse and Maya move to Boulevard Henry IV. Picasso visits them on weekends. His sculptor's studio is in his bathroom.

1942—On June 21, he becomes Maya's godfather because he could never give her his name.

1943—Picasso assembles *Head of a Bull*, a bike seat as the head; its handles are the bull's horns. In May, he meets Françoise Gilot.

1944—Picasso joins the Communist Party after the liberation of Paris on August 25. Dora goes to the Hôpital Sainte-Anne to undergo psychiatric treatment.

1945—Picasso spends July in Antibes with Dora. He rents a room for Françoise in the vicinity, but she goes to Brittany. He buys Dora a house in Ménerbes and pays for it with a still life. He begins working on lithographs. On May 5, he paints *La Femme Fleur.*

1946—Françoise moves in with Pablo. He takes her to Ménerbes, where they stay with Dora. Picasso works at Château Grimaldi in Antibes and donates pictures to the museum, soon renamed Musée Picasso.

1947—On May 15, Françoise gives birth to their son Claude. Picasso makes ceramics at the Madoura pottery, creating 2000 pieces between 1947 and 1948.

1948—Picasso moves with Françoise and Claude to La Galloise in Vallauris. Pablo takes part in the Congress of Intellectuals for Peace in Wroclaw, Poland.

1949—*Dove* lithograph becomes the motif for the poster announcing the World Peace Conference in Paris. On April 19, Françoise gives birth to their daughter Paloma. Picasso buys La Galloise from Françoise.

1950—Picasso receives his first Lenin Peace Prize. He helps Fernande, who has now become homeless.

1951—Picasso sculpts *Baboon and Young*. Claude's toy cars form the baboon's head.

1953—Picasso takes Maya and Paulo to Perpignan, where he meets Jacqueline Roque. Françoise moves with her children to 9, rue Gay-Lussac in Paris.

1954—Picasso spends time in Vallauris with Françoise, his children, and Jacqueline.

1955—On February 11, Olga dies of cancer. Françoise marries Luc Simon. Pablo buys La Californie in Cannes.

1958—Picasso buys Château Vauvenargues near Aix-en-Provence.

1959—Picasso petitions the Minister of Justice to give his name to Maya, Claude, and Paloma.

1960—Françoise divorces Luc Simon, but they remain friends.

1961—On March 2, Picasso marries Jacqueline Roque in Vallauris. They move to Notre Dame-de-Vie in Mougins.

1962—Picasso receives his second Lenin Peace Prize.

1963—The Picasso Museum opens in Barcelona.

1964— The publication of Françoise Guilot's memoir, *Life with Picasso*, results in a rift between Picasso and their children, Claude and Paloma.

1965—Picasso's lawsuit against Françoise for *Life with Picasso* is dismissed.

1966—On January 29, Fernande Olivier dies.

1970—Françoise marries Dr. Jonas Salk, best known for his discovery and development of the first safe and effective polio vaccine.

1973—On April 8, Picasso dies at Mas-Notre-Dame-de-Vie in Mougins. On April 10, he is buried on the grounds of Château Vauvenargues. On the day after Picasso's burial, his grandson Pablito drinks bleach and dies three days later.

1974—On June 6, Maya, Claude, and Paloma are officially recognized as the natural children of Pablo Picasso.

1975—On June 5, Paulo dies of liver cancer.

1977—On October 19, Marie-Thérèse Walter hangs herself in the garage of her house in Juan les-Pins. She is buried in Antibes.

1985—The Picasso Museum in Paris opens.

1986—On October 15, Jacqueline Roque shoots herself on the head with a revolver. She is buried with Picasso in Vauvenargues.

1997—On July 16, Dora Maar dies.

2003—In October, the Picasso Museum opens in Málaga.

2010—Françoise speaks in a video about her relationship with Picasso.

GLOSSARY

Abuela: Grandmother
Banderillero: Bullfighter who sticks the darts on the bull's neck.
Belle: Beautiful
Cieux!: Heavens!
Concha: Shell
Corridas: Bullfights
Guiterre: Title of one of many of Picasso's abstract compositions representing a guitar.
Je t'aime: I love you
Les Demoiselles d'Avignon: The Women of Avignon
Ma Jolie: My pretty
Malagueña: Woman from Málaga, Spain
Matadores: Bullfighters who kill the bull
ménage à trois: Threesome relationship
Mirada fuerte: Andalusian term used for a strong gaze
Mírame que ya me miras: Look at me because you want to look at me
Novia: Sweetheart
¡Olé!: Bravo, well-done
Paloma: Dove
Parroquia de Santiago: Parish of Saint James
Picadores: Horsemen in a bullfight who prick the bull to help make its head stay down.
Tía: Aunt
Tío: Uncle
Toréador: Although this song is not always played at bullfights, it has been chosen here to honor the toreador song in Georges Bizet's French opera *Carmen.*
Torrija: Fritter topped with syrup
Traje de luces: "Suit of Lights", bullfighter suit
¡Triquitraque!: Sound, clatter
¡Vale!: Okay!
Verde: Green
Yo: I
Zarzuelas: Traditional Spanish operettas

SOURCES

Balsassari, Anne. *Picasso: Life with Dora Maar.* Paris: Flammarion, 2006.
Brassaï. *Conversations with Picasso.* Chicago: The University of Chicago Press, 1999.
Duncan, David Douglas. *Goodbye Picasso.* New York: Grosset & Dunlap, 1974.
Duncan, David Douglas. *The Private World of Pablo Picasso.* New York: The Ridge Press, 1958.
Gilot, Françoise and Lake, Carlton. *Life with Picasso.* New York: Anchor Books, 1989.
Huffington, Arianna Stassinopoulos. *Picasso: Creator and Destroyer.* New York: Avon Books, 1988.
Inglada, Rafael. *Picasso: Antes del azul.* Málaga: Fundación Picasso, 2003.
Jaffe, Hans Ludwig C. *Picasso.* New York: Harry N. Abrams, Inc., 2000.
Olivier, Fernande. *Loving Picasso: The Private Journal of Fernande Olivier.* New York: Harry N. Abrams Inc., Publishers, 2000.
On-line Picasso Project http://picasso.shsu.edu
Otero, Roberto. *Forever Picasso.* New York: Harry N. Abrams Inc., Publishers, 1974.
Picasso, Marina. *Picasso: My Grandfather.* New York: Riverhead Books, 2001.
Richardson, John. *A Life of Picasso: The Cubist Rebel 1907-1916.* New York: Alfred A. Knopf, 2007.
Richardson, John. *A Life of Picasso: The Prodigy 1881-1906.* New York: Alfred A. Knopf, 2007.
Richardson, John. *A Life of Picasso: The Triumphant Years 1917-1932.* New York: Alfred A. Knopf, 2007.
Rose, Charlie. "A Conversation about 'Picasso Mosqueteros' with John Richardson and Bernard Picasso." www.charlierose.com/view/interview/10183
Stein, Gertrude. *Picasso.* New York: Dover Publications, 1984.
Widmaier Picasso, Olivier. *Picasso: The Real Family Story.* New York: Prestel, 2004.

NOTES

"My grandfather was a Sun": Widmaier Picasso, *Picasso: The Real Family Story*, p. 23.
"Painting is poetry": Gilot, *Life with Picasso*, p. 120.

A Prodigy
"If you become a soldier": Paraphrase, Gilot, *Life with Picasso*, p. 60.

Blue Baby
11:15: At times, Picasso said he was born at 9:30 PM. His baptismal register says 11:15.
Tío: Doctor Salvador Ruiz, Picasso's father's brother
Christened: On November 10, 1881, Pablo, after his dead uncle; Diego, after his paternal grandfather and eldest uncle;
    José, after his father; Francisco de Paula, after his maternal grandfather; Juan Nepomuceno, after his godfather; María
    de los Remedios, after his godmother; Cipriano, because he was born on St. Crispin Day; de la Santísima Trinidad (the
    Most Holy Trinity), the most holy first name always at the end of a Spanish name; Ruiz y Picasso, after his father and
    mother's surnames, the mother's surname always at the end of a Spanish name.

Sun King
"An angel and a devil": Huffington, *Picasso*, p. 19.
Abuela: Maternal grandmother Doña Inés Picasso
Two *tías*: Elaida and Heliodora came to live with them after the devastation of their vineyards by the phylloxera pest. They
    made braids for railroad workers' uniforms.
"Piz": Richardson, *A Life of Picasso: The Prodigy*, p. 27.

Mama: Doña María Picasso y López
Mama: María was twenty-six when Picasso was born.

Papa: Don José Ruiz y Blasco
Papa: Don José, curator of a museum in Málaga, was forty-one when Pablo was born.
Cara Ancha: José Sánchez del Campo, famous torero

In the Mist of Aftershocks
Artist who owns a stone house: Antonio Muñoz Degrain was in Rome. Degrain's wife was at home.
Lola: María de los Dolores

Arithmetic Art
School: Pablo attended Saint Raphael.

His Audience
Conchita: María de la Concepción
"What do you want me": Paraphrase, Richardson, *A Life of Picasso: The Prodigy*, p. 31.

Vow to God
A Coruña: "A Coruña" in Galician and "La Coruña" in Spanish. Don José moved his family to this Spanish city by the
    Atlantic Ocean when he lost his job in Málaga.
"I vow": Paraphrase, Richardson, *A Life of Picasso: The Prodigy*, p. 49.

Set Him Free
La Llotja in Catalan (La Lonja in Spanish): the School of Fine Arts in Barcelona
Commissioned painting: *Christ Appearing to Blessed Marguerite Marie Alacoque*
"The idea bores me": Richardson, *A Life of Picasso: The Prodigy*, p. 73.
Manuel Pallarés: classmate in La Llotja who introduced Pablo to the brothels and sometimes paid for his prostitutes.
"You're taking the wrong road": Richardson, *A Life of Picasso: The Prodigy*, p. 95. Don José also said this because Pablo was
    imitating El Greco, who wasn't considered a great artist.

Gypsy Boy

Horta de Ebro: Today Horta de Saint Joan. Picasso's classmate Pallarés took him to Horta to recover from scarlet fever.

"Whatever I know I learned": Huffington, *Picasso: Creator and Destroyer*, p. 41.

Pallarés denies the story, but Picasso said that he was in love with the gypsy. The gypsy might have been Fabián de Castro, an artist who lived in Bateau-Lavoir.

I the King

"One portrait: 10 pesetas": Richardson, *A Life of Picasso: The Prodigy*, p. 156.

"*Yo*": Ibid., p. 148.

"*Yo el rey*, I the King": Ibid., p. 156.

La Belle Fernande

Fernande Olivier: Her real name was Amélie Lang. Her father's name is unknown, but it might have been Bellevalé, a surname she briefly adopted and sometimes spelled Belvallé or Belvalet. Picasso kept in boxes large numbers of beautiful drawings done by her. She earned her living by posing for artists.

"You can have people": Rose, "A Conversation about Picasso"

Mírame: Excerpts of Picasso's poem "XVIII" Part: 2 (January 20, 1936) http://picasso.shsu.edu/index.php?view=WritingsInfo&mid=52&year=1936&part=2

Gertrude Stein

"I am alone": Stein, *Picasso*, back cover.

"Nobody thinks it is": Jaffe, *Picasso*, p. 78.

"Little by little": Stein, *Picasso*, p. 7.

Les Demoiselles d' Avignon

Avignon: This was a street of brothels. The painting used to have a medical student as a symbol of death and a sailor as a customer. Picasso painted over them.

Intercessors: "The Africans were 'intercessors'...against anything: against unfamiliar or threatening spirits... If you give spirits a form then you become independent."

Widmaier Picasso, *Picasso: The Real Family Story*, pp. 290-291.

I Picasso

I Picasso: In 1901 Picasso painted his self-portrait and entitled it *Yo Picasso*.

"Every time I draw a man": Brassaï, *Conversations with Picasso*, p. 66.

Cubism with Cubes

"What a loss": Henri Matisse when he saw *Les Demoiselles d'Avignon*. Richardson, *A Life of Picasso: The Cubist Rebel*, p. 106. Gertrude Stein attributes the phrase to Russian collector Tschoukine. Stein, *Picasso*, p. 18.

"I want an engineer": Huffington, *Picasso: Creator and Destroyer*, p. 98.

Pioneers of Cubism

"Almost every evening": Gilot, *Life with Picasso*, p. 76.

Madame Picasso

Rises high: The Steins buy seven Picassos, Ambroise Vollard buys twenty.

"Are you upset": Paraphrase, Olivier, *Loving Picasso*, p. 265.

"I'm thinking": Ibid.

Raymonde: In April 1907 Fernande and Picasso went to the orphanage in the rue Caulaincourt. In July, Fernande returned Raymonde to the orphanage. That prompted Fernande and Picasso to separate between June and September. They got back together from 1907 to 1912. They separated for good when Picasso met Eva.

Cursed

Newspaper: *Excelsior*

Eva Guel: Her real name was Marcelle Humbert. She also went by Eva Markous.

Breast cancer: Some books state that it was throat cancer. Fernande said she cursed Eva.

"I love you in every color": Richardson, *Picasso: The Cubist Rebel*, p. 367.

"*Je t'aime Gaby*": Ibid.

Gaby la Catalane: Cabaret singer and dancer Gaby Depeyre was also the lover of American engraver and poet Herbert Lespinasse, whom she married.

Gold Crowns

Parade: One-act ballet. In love with Picasso, writer Jean Cocteau begged him to come to Rome.

Wedding day: They had planned to marry in April but postponed it when Olga had surgery on her right foot.

Wedding witnesses: Picasso's poet friends: Jean Cocteau, Guillaume Apollinaire, and Max Jacob. Olga didn't like Jacob because he was in love with Picasso.

Paris apartment: French Regency style apartment in rue La Boétie

Car: a Panhard-Levassor. Later Picasso bought a Hispano-Suiza.

Paolo

Paulo: Paul Joseph, sometimes called Paulot.

Tutor: It wasn't until Paulo was ten that Olga consented to send him to Hattemer School in Paris.

Tangle of Amorous Liaison

"Mademoiselle": Widmaier Picasso, *Picasso: The Real Family Story*, p. 51.

"Come back tomorrow": Ibid.

Studio: Picasso's sculpture studio was in the stables of Château Boisgeloup which had no electricity. At night he worked using a large oil lamp or the lights of his car. He intended to make the château Marie-Thérèse's residency. Fate ruled otherwise.

Knife Game

Dora Maar: Her real name was Theodora Markovitch. Poet Paul Eluard introduced her to Picasso at the café Les Deux-Magots. Yugoslav from her father's side and French from her mother's, Dora had lived in Argentina and spoke fluent Spanish.

Young beautiful carpenter: Baldassari, *Picasso: Life with Dora Maar*, p. 36.

Weeping Woman

"What a surprise!": Widmaier Picasso, *Picasso: The Real Family Story*, p. 65.

May patience: Baldassari, *Picasso: Life with Dora Maar*, p. 128.

"Things have changed": Widmaier Picasso, *Picasso: The Real Family Story*, p. 65.

"Come, come, my dear": Ibid.

"Do you love me?": Ibid.

"Dora Maar, you know": Ibid.

World War II

Paris: Picasso had invitations and money to leave Paris. He could have gone to Mexico, Brazil, or the United States. He stayed.

"Degenerate": Baldassari, *Picasso: Life with Dora Maar*, p. 240.

"Did you do that?": Ibid.

La Femme-Fleur/ The Flower Woman

Françoise Gilot: Picasso met her while he was dining with Dora in Le Catalan, a small restaurant opposite his studio on the rue des Grands-Augustins.

Verde-leaf hair: Henri Matisse had said that he would paint Françoise in green, so jealous Picasso painted her that way.

"It's strange, isn't it?": Gilot, *Pablo Picasso: The Time with Françoise Gilot*, p. 23.

Love Oath

"You're going to swear": Gilot, *Life with Picasso*, p. 134.

Claude: Named after Claude Gillot, painter of harlequins.

Paloma: means "dove." Paloma was born when Picasso was at the World Peace Conference in Paris. His lithograph made the dove a peace symbol.

"I Am God"

"God is really another artist": Gilot, *Life with Picasso*, p. 50.

"I am God": Richardson, *A Life of Picasso: The Prodigy*, p. 463.

Orbiting the King

Stalk: Olga also stalked Françoise and sometimes even pinched her.

"If you go on living": Paraphrase, Gilot, *Life with Picasso*, p. 89.

"Why do you want": Ibid., p. 130.

"No woman leaves": Ibid., p. 354.

Françoise: Moved with her children to Picasso's apartment on rue Gay Lussac in Paris. She enrolled the children in L'École Alsacienne. She didn't accept any alimony from Picasso. Today she gives talks about his art.

Blank Canvas

Olga's death: She had a stroke that paralyzed her legs, but she refused a wheelchair. She died in a nursing home in Cannes.

"It's too late": Widmaier Picasso, *Picasso: The Real Family Story*, p. 197.

Jacqueline Roque

"One can't leave": Gilot, *Life with Picasso*, p. 358.

Jacqueline helped with sales at the Galerie Madoura in Vallauris. She lived in Antibes in the Ziquet villa, the reason a portrait of Jacqueline bears the title *Madame Z*.

Cathy: Catherine Hutin

Villa La Californie

Roman arenas: In Arles and Nîmes

"This landscape belongs to me.": Brassaï, *Conversations with Picasso*, p. 261.

Bullfight

"He made a mistake": Duncan, *The Private World of Pablo Picasso*, p. 82.

Jacqueline's Sun

"I bet you can't guess": Otero, *Forever Picasso*, p. 62.

"I have less and less time": Gilot, *Life with Picasso*, p. 124.

"I have less and less time": Gilot, *Life with Picasso*, p. 124.

Jacqueline de Vauvenargues: Portrait by Picasso.

"The sun doesn't want": Picasso, Marina, *Picasso: My grandfather*, p. 7

Hommage â Picasso

"Just what I needed": Otero, *Forever Picasso*, p. 75.

"How was it?": Ibid., p. 161.

"There are a lot of paintings": Ibid.

"To tell you the truth": Ibid., p. 162.

Bull Kills Matador

"I paint as others would write": Widmaier Picasso, *Picasso: The Real Family Story*, p. 303.

She calls him: Marie-Thérèse phoned Picasso eight days before his death.

"Everything approaches": Widmaier Picasso, *Picasso: The Real Family Story*, p. 285.

Pablo Picasso and the Mistress Who Never Left Him

"The Painter": Widmaier Picasso, *Picasso: The Real Family Story*, pp. 7-8.

"He was born among the dead": Ibid., p. 286.

"I think of it from morning": Ibid., p. 298.

"I saw that Picasso": Ibid., p. 59.

"My God if you only knew": Gilot, *Life with Picasso*, p. 155.

"The reward for love": Widmaier Picasso, *Picasso: The Real Family Story*, p. 151.

"When I die": Picasso, Marina, *Picasso: My Grandfather*, p. 183.